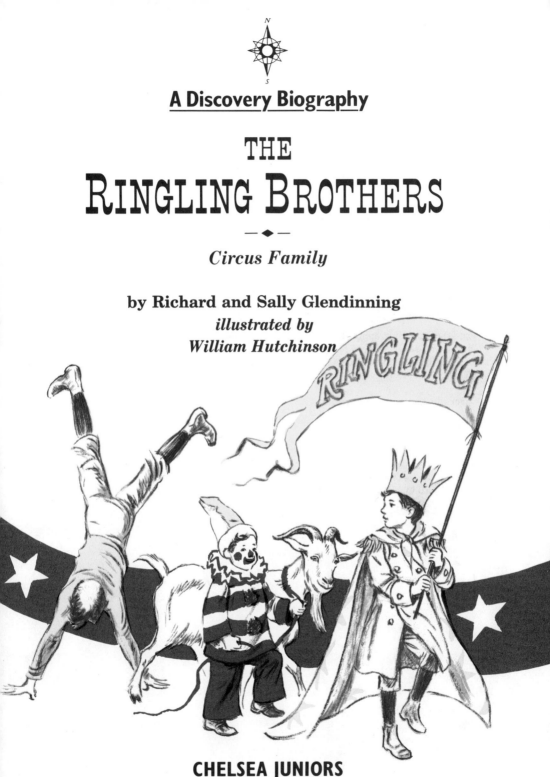

A Discovery Biography

THE
RINGLING BROTHERS
—◆—

Circus Family

by Richard and Sally Glendinning
illustrated by
William Hutchinson

CHELSEA JUNIORS
A division of Chelsea House Publishers
New York ◆ Philadelphia

JB RING

To our daughter Ann

The Discovery Biographies have been prepared under the
educational supervision of Mary C. Austin, Ed.D.,
Reading Specialist and Professor of Education, Case
Western Reserve University.

Cover illustration: Lisa Desimini

First Chelsea House edition 1991

1 3 5 7 9 8 6 4 2

ISBN 0-7910-1468-1

1. Ringling Brothers – Juvenile Literature

Contents

The Ringling Brothers: Circus Family

Chapter 1

The Circus Boat

Five Ringling boys waited by the river on a May morning in 1870. The sun would not rise for another hour. The air was damp and cold. The boys kept their eyes on the dark waters of the river. They were watching for the big circus boat!

The boys lived near the river in the small town of McGregor, Iowa. Few shows of any kind ever came to McGregor.

"Will the circus boat come soon?"

asked four-year-old John Ringling. He was the youngest of the five brothers.

Eighteen-year-old Al, the oldest of the boys, patted John's curly head. "Papa said the boat would dock here before sunrise," he said kindly.

The other three boys were Otto, Alf T., and Charlie. Otto stood still, but Alf T. and Charlie danced about to keep their feet warm as they waited for the boat.

Other boys and their fathers were coming down the path to the river. They carried lanterns to light the way. They shouted greetings to the Ringling boys.

Soon they heard the steam whistles of the circus boat. Al lifted little John high on his shoulders. "Now you can see the boat when it comes to the dock," Al said.

"I can see it now!" John shouted, waving his arms. "The circus boat looks bigger than a house!"

The great white steamboat carried the whole circus from one town to another along the river. It shone in the golden light of pine torches and lanterns on the decks. Red and blue pennants flapped in the breeze. Now the boat moved toward the dock. Strong men began to move trunks and boxes to the deck for unloading.

"Down with the main gangplank!" called the captain.

"Down with the gangplank!" the workers shouted in reply as they lowered the gangplank to the dock.

Men with lanterns led teams of horses ashore. Other circus animals and performers followed. A brown bear with a ring in his nose stood on his hind feet as he was led away. Then came a huge gray animal.

"That must be the elephant!" John screamed in joy. "It looks just like the picture of an elephant that papa showed me!"

The elephant stood still for a moment. His big ears flapped back and forth like huge fans. His trunk waved slowly from side to side.

The Ringling boys stared in wonder at the big animal. They were afraid the gangplank would break when the elephant stepped on it. But the elephant slowly walked down it to the dock. "He made it! He made it!" cried John.

After the circus was unloaded, the Ringling brothers went home. Mama Ringling had their breakfast all ready. They enjoyed a good breakfast. Then they ran to the main street to wait for the circus parade.

"I can't see anything!" cried little John, as men and women moved in front of him on the sidewalk. Once more, Al lifted John to his shoulders.

Everybody cheered as the circus parade moved down the street. The owner of the circus led the way in a shiny black buggy. Next came the bandwagon, pulled by a team of spotted ponies. The men in the band wore uniforms of red and gold. Their golden horns flashed as they played one tune after another.

A dozen men and women riding on horseback followed the bandwagon. They wore gay costumes of silver and yellow and blue. The horses pranced in time to the music, snorting and tossing their heads.

"What beautiful horses they are!" said Al Ringling. Al loved animals even more than the other boys did.

"Here comes the clown!" cried Charlie and Alf T.

The clown sat in a small cart pulled by a donkey. The Ringling boys waved, and the clown waved back.

"Everybody in the circus looks so happy," Al said to his brothers. "It must be fun to work for a circus."

"I wish we could join the circus," sighed Otto.

"Maybe we could start a circus of our own someday," Al said.

"We'd never save enough money to start a circus," Otto replied. "Why, we don't even have money enough to buy tickets for this circus."

The boys knew their father couldn't

buy tickets for them. Papa Ringling worked hard to earn enough to feed and clothe his family.

When the boys got home after the parade, Papa Ringling had a surprise for them.

"I mended a leather belt for one of the circus performers," papa told the boys. He held up a piece of paper. "The man gave me this ticket to the circus!" papa said.

The boys looked at one another. They said nothing, for they were wondering who would be the lucky person to use the ticket.

Papa Ringling's eyes twinkled as he watched them. At last he said, "Boys, this is a family ticket! Now the whole Ringling family can go to the circus!"

The boys could hardly believe that

such good luck had come their way. Soon they went to the field where the circus tent stood. Papa Ringling handed the ticket to a man at the door. All the Ringlings went inside. They sat with others on a long wooden bench to watch the show.

A whistle blew, and the show began. The clown sang funny songs. The men in the band played one tune after another, and the clown danced to the music.

A big man entered the ring. He wore a wide leather belt with a small metal cup at one side. "That's the man who gave me the circus ticket," Papa Ringling whispered to the boys. "He's wearing the belt I mended for him."

The man rested a long pole in the metal cup on his belt. He held onto the pole while an acrobat climbed to the top. He held the pole steady as the acrobat twisted and turned high in the air. The Ringling boys gasped as the acrobat seemed about to lose his hold on the pole. They shouted as he finished his act safely.

The five Ringling brothers loved everything about the circus. They wanted to join the laughing performers whose tricks looked so easy. They wanted to paint their faces, put on funny clothes, and tell jokes with the clown. They wanted to blow horns like the men in the band. They wanted to ride on the dancing horses. How wonderful it would be to have even a small circus!

Chapter 2

Backyard Circus

August Ringling, the boys' father, was born in Germany. There he learned the trade of harness-making. He cut thin strips of leather to make the reins and bridles for horses that pulled fine carriages and buggies. He made big leather collars for horses.

He even learned to cut and sew the leather tops and side curtains for buggies and carriages. Harness-making and carriage-trimming were needed skills at that time.

August Ringling had left his home

in Germany as a young man to seek his fortune in America. He thought that perhaps in America a good harness-maker could open a shop of his own. While working in Milwaukee, Wisconsin, he met and married pretty Marie Salomé Juliar.

"Perhaps I could make more money in a smaller town," he told his wife.

They moved to the little town of Baraboo, Wisconsin, and lived there for five years. Then they moved to McGregor, Iowa, a fast-growing town on the Mississippi River. Papa Ringling opened his own shop.

Al Ringling was the oldest son. Every two or three years a new baby arrived, until Papa and Mama Ringling had seven sons. After Al came Gus, then Otto, Alf T., Charlie, John, and Henry.

Gus, the second son, was away from home visiting a friend in another town when the circus boat arrived. Henry was only a baby, so he missed all the circus fun.

The other five boys never forgot the riverboat circus. They began to plan for a small show of their own.

"Papa, could we use the empty room in the stable to get ready for our show?" Al asked his father.

"I guess that will be all right," papa said.

From then on, the stable room was filled with the five Ringling boys and their friends. The younger boys practiced cartwheels and handstands. They turned somersaults backward and forward. They kept at it day after day, and soon they became very good acrobats.

Al tried something more difficult. He wanted to be a juggler. He tried to juggle wooden barrel hoops as a man in the circus had done. He tossed the barrel hoops into the air with one hand and tried to catch them with the other. At first the barrel hoops clattered to the ground. Al became more skillful as he tossed the hoops into the air again and again. At last he could keep several hoops whirling one after another without dropping any of them.

On sunny afternoons the boys practiced their circus acts in the backyard. Neighbors gathered to watch them. They laughed at roly-poly little John who tumbled about trying to imitate his older brothers.

Only Henry and Gus failed to join in the fun. Henry was too young, and Gus didn't share his brothers' dream of having a circus. Besides, he now had a job that kept him busy. The large family needed the money he earned.

One day Papa Ringling came home leading an old horse. It was a bony, sad-eyed, swaybacked old animal, but it *was* a horse!

"Now we have a real horse for our circus!" Alf T. shouted.

"Oh, papa, now we can learn to ride bareback like the people we saw in the circus!" cried Charlie.

"Harumph," papa grumbled. "I bought the horse to pull the plow for our garden." Then he smiled at the boys. "Maybe you can ride bareback after you plow the garden."

The Ringling boys took good care of the old horse. Charlie and Alf T.

led him to a field where the grass was thick. They brought him apples and carrots to eat. Otto brushed away at the horse's rough coat to make it silky and shining.

What fun the boys had learning to ride! The old horse was gentle. The boys taught him to go round and round in a circle, just as the horses had done in the circus ring. One after another, the boys learned to leap onto the horse's back and hang onto his mane. Sometimes they toppled off and fell to the ground, but that didn't spoil the fun. Riding the old horse was almost like having a real circus right in their own backyard.

Chapter *3*

Circus in McGregor

Nearly a year had gone by since the five Ringling brothers went to the circus. They had given many little shows in their own backyard. They put up old blankets on lines between trees for a circus tent. Each new performance was better than the one before.

"I know where we can get an old wagon," Otto told his brothers one day. "We could use it in our next circus."

The boys had no money to spend.

They traded everything they had— their pocketknives, a broken watch, and a leaky boat—for the wagon. They scraped off the old paint and fixed the broken wheels. Then they painted the wagon bright red and yellow.

Papa Ringling made a harness for the old horse so that he could pull the wagon.

"I know where we can get another animal for our circus," Otto said one day. "I saw a goat down near the big stable where a man has horses to rent. I don't think the goat belongs to anybody."

The owner of the stable told the boys to take the goat home. He was happy to be rid of him. The boys named the goat Billy Rainbow. They tried to train him to do some easy tricks, but he didn't always obey. Like most goats, he was stubborn.

While the other boys worked with Billy Rainbow, Al practiced juggling. He had become a very good juggler. Now he practiced with balls of string, old hats, and even with his mother's second-best china plates.

"Al, you have broken so many plates that soon we will have none left to eat from," mama scolded. She wasn't really angry. She liked to see her boys busy and happy together. She wished, however, that they would spend more time on their school lessons.

The Ringling house was a noisy place in the evenings. Somebody had given Al an old bugle which he learned to play well. Alf T. and Charlie also taught themselves to play the bugle. They even made up little tunes of their own.

The brothers practiced hard on any musical instruments they could find. They blew on tin whistles and on combs wrapped in thin paper. Otto, who could never carry a tune, banged away on a drum. John liked to sing in his high, little-boy voice.

They began to get ready for their first real circus. They planned to have costumes, music, and a real circus tent. A kind man gave them some cardboard from which they made big signs to tell people about their circus. They cut up some of the cardboard to use as tickets.

The boys had earned a little money from their backyard shows. They gave all the money to Otto so they wouldn't waste it on candy or small

trinkets. Plump, quiet Otto learned how to save money even as a boy. When grown-ups gave the boys a few pennies or a nickel from time to time, the money went into Otto's box.

At last they had saved eight dollars. They spent the money to buy cloth for a tent which mama helped them sew.

The sun shone bright on the day of their big parade. People gathered along the street to watch the Ringling boys and their friends go by.

The old horse pulled the red and yellow wagon. Al sat in the wagon. He held the reins between his knees and blew on the bugle as loud as he could.

Next came Otto and Billy Rainbow. Otto had rubbed the goat's long horns with oil to make them shine.

He had even brushed the goat's long chin whiskers. Alf T. and Charlie marched gaily along, one with a tin whistle, the other with a mouth organ. John was last in the parade. He scampered along on his short little legs to keep up with the others. John wore a clown suit Mama Ringling had made for him.

"Come to see the circus!" the boys shouted to the people on the street. "Come to see the big Ringling Circus in the tent!"

Other boys marched in the parade. They waved banners with the word "Ringling" printed on them in big letters.

The crowd followed the parade to a vacant lot near the drugstore. The boys had put up their tent there. Otto stood in front of the tent to collect a nickel from each person who wanted to see the show.

What a show it was! Alf T. was the first to march into the tent. He wore an old soldier's uniform trimmed with brass buttons and gold braid. A cape made from a patchwork quilt hung from his shoulders. He wore a gold paper crown on his head. Alf T. walked proudly, the way he imagined a real king would walk.

The next performer to enter the tent was five-year-old John in his clown suit. John was trying to lead Billy Rainbow, but the old goat had some new tricks in mind.

Billy Rainbow broke loose! He pawed the ground. He put his head down and rubbed his shiny horns in the dirt. "Baa-a-a—" bleated Billy Rainbow. His chin whiskers shook.

Then Billy Rainbow butted Alf T. so hard that the gold paper crown fell off. Alf T. fell forward on his hands and knees. The patchwork cape became tangled in the goat's horns. Billy Rainbow tossed his head and pawed at the cape until it tore apart and dropped to the ground.

The audience roared with laughter. Alf T. got up and rubbed the seat of his pants. He tried to put the crown back on his head, but it was bent.

Then Al came into the tent. He began his juggling act. He was nervous, because this was his first performance before a big audience. His hands shook a little. He made several mistakes. The crowd laughed when Al dropped two of his mother's plates. He tried to pick up all the pieces from the ground. The crowd laughed harder.

Everything seemed to go wrong. Charlie tried to do some tricks on the old horse's back, but he kept falling to the ground. John sang a funny song, rolling his eyes from side to side.

It was a good show in spite of the mistakes the boys made. The people in the audience didn't mind the mistakes, and everybody had a good time.

Papa Ringling said to his wife that evening, "It was a good little circus. I am proud of our sons. Now that the show is over, maybe they will turn to their school books again, or to helping me in the harness shop."

Mama Ringling shook her head. "I heard the boys talking after supper," she said. "Already they are making plans for their next circus."

Chapter *4*

The Icehouse Circus

One year after the Ringling boys gave their circus, Papa Ringling decided it was time to move again. A new carriage factory had been built in the town of Prairie du Chien, Wisconsin. Papa and Al could work there, making the leather tops and side curtains for carriages.

All of the Ringlings except Gus moved to Prairie du Chien. Gus had to stay at his job in McGregor. Otto, Alf T., Charlie, and John went to school. Their minds were not on

their lessons. They could hardly wait
for school to end each day, so that
they could plan for the next circus.

One evening they waited for Al to
come home from the factory. They ran
to meet him.

"We found a good place to hold
our next circus," Otto called out.

"It's an old icehouse, with plenty
of room inside," said Alf T.

There were no refrigerators then.
Men cut blocks of ice from frozen
lakes and streams and stored the
blocks in icehouses. They sold the
blocks of ice during the summer.

"This time we'll have more animals
in our show," said John. Besides the
horse and Billy Rainbow, the boys now
had a live rattlesnake in a cage.
They also had a badger they had
trapped in the woods.

Al, now 20 years old, planned the show carefully. "This time we must give a really good performance," he said. "People had a fine time at our circus in McGregor because we made them laugh. We must still make people laugh at our jokes and funny songs. But we also want to scare them when we try daring tricks."

Al made a trapeze from a wooden bar and two pieces of rope. He hung it from the rafters in a barn near the Ringling house. The younger boys learned to hang by their knees and swing to and fro on the trapeze. They also learned other tricks.

Al had become an expert in acrobatics and in juggling. Now he wanted to learn tightrope walking.

He strung a rope between two trees a few inches above the ground.

He fell from the rope many times as he tried to walk across it. But it was not long before he could walk the length of rope without falling. Then he raised the rope a few inches higher. At last he felt quite safe high in the air, with only the rope under his feet.

A large audience came to see the circus in the icehouse. People had heard that the five Ringling brothers could give a show almost as good as a real traveling circus. All of the boys did well, but Al was the star.

The audience was silent as Al climbed a tall ladder. People stared at the rope stretched high in the air from one wall to another. Could Al Ringling really walk across the rope? Al bowed to the audience. Then he began the walk high up in the air, putting one foot carefully in front of the other.

When he reached the center of the rope, he teetered on one foot as if he were about to fall. The crowd gasped.

"Al really looks as if he's about to fall," whispered John.

"Don't be silly," Otto answered. "Don't you remember? Al practiced this part about nearly falling. It makes his tightrope walking look so much harder."

Sure enough, Al did regain his balance. He almost danced on the rope the rest of the way. Cheers broke out as Al made it safely to the other side.

"That young man is better than any circus performer I ever saw," said someone in the audience.

The circus in the icehouse was the

last of the Ringlings' happy times in Prairie du Chien. Soon afterward the carriage factory burned to the ground. Papa and Al were out of work.

The Ringlings moved from their big house to an old log cabin on the other side of town. It was here that the last baby, a little girl named Ida, was born. Al found a job in a carriage shop in a town some miles away. He left his job to work in shows whenever he had a chance.

Papa Ringling opened a little shop, but there was hardly any business. Times were hard, and few people had any money to spend.

Otto helped his father in the shop. The younger boys and the old horse had to work together in the garden so there would be enough food for the family.

Chapter 5

The Hall Show

The years passed, but the five Ringling brothers never forgot the circus boat they had seen long ago. They talked of the fun they had had in planning their own shows.

Four years after the icehouse circus, the Ringlings moved back to Baraboo. The boys were growing up to be strong, handsome young men. Al and Otto had jobs in other places, so the family was no longer together.

"I guess we'll never have another circus," Alf T. said to Charlie. "Papa needs us to help in the harness shop."

"You're right," Charlie said sadly. Then his face brightened. "At least, we can keep on with our music. We might be able to earn some money that way."

Charlie practiced on the violin and trombone. Alf T. liked to play the cornet. Both of them became good musicians. They joined other boys in forming a small dance band.

Al Ringling soon got his first full-time job in a real show. Later he acted as its manager. He also performed as an acrobat and a juggler, and sometimes he played in the band. During the winter months, the show went from one small town to another. It was called a hall show, for it was given in public rooms or halls. Al was nearly 30 years old when he decided that he and his brothers could give their own hall show.

Alf T., Charlie, and John were eager to start. Otto wrote that he would quit his job and join them soon.

"I've written a few short plays," Alf T. said. "Maybe we could give a play as part of the show."

"Great!" said Al. "Let's start to plan the program now."

"Whatever it is, I'm ready!" John said eagerly. John was a big fellow now, nearly sixteen years old. He had never liked going to school, and he hated the work in papa's harness shop.

"What can you do, John?" asked Al.

"I can sing songs and tell jokes,"

John said. "And I can make people laugh."

Al frowned. "That's not enough," he said. "We'll need another horn for our band."

John hung his head. "I guess I've been lazy," he said. "I never learned to play a musical instrument like the rest of you fellows."

"Then you can learn now," Al said firmly. He handed one of Charlie's horns to John. "Go upstairs and blow away on this horn. I'll just lock you in so you won't run off."

John spent many hours behind the locked door. He blew away on the horn. At first he could make only a few squawking sounds. But at last he learned to play well enough to join his brothers.

Papa Ringling didn't like the idea

of the hall show. He wanted his boys to find steady jobs and settle down. He could do nothing to stop the older boys, but he refused to let John go.

"John is too young," papa said. "I want him to stay at home and finish high school."

John stormed and shouted. He said he would run away from home. Papa remained firm. Al, Alf T., and Charlie left home without John.

The three brothers gave the first of the Ringling hall shows in towns so small that no other shows came there. Sometimes only a few people bought tickets for the show. There was barely enough money to pay for train tickets to the next town. The three brothers often slept on benches in the waiting room at railroad

stations. They had no money to spend on rooms in a hotel.

Still, they were happy working together in real shows. Their letters home were filled with stories of their adventures.

John made such a fuss at home that he was finally permitted to join his brothers. A few weeks later, Otto left his job to travel with the show. The five performing Ringling brothers were together again!

One night they gave a show in a big meeting room at a hotel. Men, women, and children crowded into the room.

First came the band music by the five brothers and two young musicians who worked for them. Al and Alf T. tootled away on cornets, and Charlie blew hard into his long trombone.

John played more softly on his horn, in hopes nobody would hear if he played a wrong note. Otto thumped on the drum.

After that, they gave the funny little play that Alf T. had written. Charlie hurried into the next room to change his costume so that he could perform acrobatic stunts.

"And now, ladies and gentlemen—" Al cried, "here is John Ringling!"

John wore a Dutch costume. He was a big fellow, nearly six feet tall. He rolled his dark eyes and waggled his head as he danced about the room in wooden shoes and sang.

"What shall I do with this?" Al asked the audience. He held up a plow for the crowd to see.

"You use it to plow a field!" the audience shouted.

"No," said Al. "I balance it on my chin!"

The audience laughed in disbelief.

Al lifted the plow carefully and tilted his chin in the air. He placed the plow on his chin. Then he walked around the room with the plow balanced on the tip of his chin.

A few minutes later, Al showed the audience a small bow like those used by Indians. In his other hand he had a long feather.

"I'll shoot the feather into the air with my bow," he cried. "How shall I catch the feather?"

"Maybe you can balance it on your chin," a small boy suggested.

"Not this time," Al laughed. "Watch and see." He shot the feather high in the air. Then he caught it on the very tip of his nose. The audience cheered and cheered as he balanced the feather on his nose.

Otto counted the money after the show was over.

"We made nearly $25 tonight," he said happily.

"Let's go out and order the biggest steaks in town," cried John. "I'm hungry!"

Otto shook his head. "We'll settle for the cheapest meal we can find, just as we always do," he said. "This money goes into our savings account at the bank."

Al nodded his head. "Otto is right," he said. "Every dollar we can save will help us buy costumes and hire people to give bigger and better shows next year. Maybe we can even save enough money to start our own circus!"

Chapter 6

Circus in Baraboo

During the winter months, the Ringling brothers traveled with their hall show. In the summer, they scattered to take any jobs they could find.

Although there was a family resemblance, the five brothers were quite different from one another. Al was the showman, always thinking of new ways to please an audience. Quiet Otto was the business manager who handled the money. Alf T. was a dreamy fellow who might have been a writer, for he loved long words. Charlie, who was not as tall as his brothers, liked to hunt and fish. Big, curly-haired John was an adventurous fellow who made friends with everybody he met.

Papa Ringling had taught his sons always to be honest in their dealings with other people. He had also taught them to work hard.

In two years, the Ringling brothers had saved $1,000 from their winter shows and summer jobs.

"We have enough money now to start a small circus," Otto told his brothers.

"Let's buy a few horses to start with," Al said. "Every circus needs animals, and I could train the horses—"

Otto shook his head. "We can't

spend money to buy horses yet," he said. "We'll have to hire a few more performers. We'll need to buy a circus tent."

Papa and Mama Ringling had moved to a distant town, and the two youngest children, Henry and Ida, went with them. Gus had been gone for many years. He was a hard worker, first as a harness-maker and later at other jobs. Although his brothers wrote many letters asking him to join them, Gus was not willing to leave a steady job for the uncertain future of a hall show and a circus.

Al, who was married now, had a small house in Baraboo. The other four brothers stayed there when they weren't traveling.

What hard work it took to start even a small circus! The Ringling brothers hired a few performers. They bought a circus tent. They went to the woods to chop down trees for tent poles. They smoothed and painted some flat boards to use for seats.

Otto and John went to nearby farms to rent horses and wagons. They needed the wagons to haul the performers, the trunks filled with costumes, the tent, and the poles from town to town.

The Ringling brothers opened their circus in Baraboo May 19, 1884. An old man named Yankee Robinson, who had owned a circus many years before, was on hand to help them.

Otto stood near the entrance to the tent. He took the tickets. He counted the money. Then he ran back of the tent to change into his band costume.

One of the hired performers called to him. "Three little boys are crawling under the tent! They are trying to get inside without paying!"

Otto frowned for a moment. He didn't want to lose the price of a single ticket. Then he smiled, as he remembered his own childhood. "Let them crawl under the tent," he said. "Maybe they don't have the money to buy tickets."

Al stood at the center of the small ring. He took off his tall hat and bowed to the crowd. Al was the ringmaster. He blew a whistle—the sign that the show was about to begin. This was the happiest moment of his life! At last the Ringling brothers had their own circus!

Just then, something happened! Some of the homemade benches fell apart. The people seated on them fell to the ground. Old Yankee Robinson ran quickly to help the people. No one was hurt, and the old showman laughed and joked as if the broken benches were part of the show. The people laughed with him.

The show started again. The brothers played in the band between their acts. Alf T. and Charlie both performed as acrobats. One of the hired performers twisted his body into strange shapes. John danced about and sang his funny songs. John was the only clown in the circus, but he made all the people laugh at his antics.

The circus in Baraboo was not very different from the hall shows the brothers had given during the winter months. The only animal act was a trained pig that danced a few steps.

Still, the performance was a success. "We're really on our way now!" Charlie said as the crowd cheered.

"I hope we can make enough money to buy a few animals soon," Al sighed. "It won't seem like a real circus until we have lots of animals."

The Ringling brothers and the hired performers took down the tent. They loaded the canvas and poles on the rented wagons.

Charlie took a last look at the vacant lot. "Everything's done!" he shouted. "We're ready to go!"

Horses pulled the rented wagons slowly down the dirt road. They moved along in a single line, each wagon following the one in front. It would take several hours to reach the nearby town where the tent would be set up for the next show.

Chapter 7

The Mud Show

Baraboo was the home town of the Ringling Circus. Year after year, the first show of the season was given there. Then the circus traveled by wagon to other small towns during the summer months. The circus season ended when autumn brought cold weather. There was no way to keep the tent warm enough for a performance.

The circus returned to Baraboo in the autumn. Young men who lived in Baraboo were hired to repair the wagons and to make new wagons for the next season. After the first year, the Ringlings had enough money to buy wagons rather than rent them.

The Ringling brothers bought strong horses to pull the wagons and other horses to perform in the circus. They bought other animals too—a striped hyena, some monkeys, two lions, a bear, and a kangaroo.

"We ought to buy an elephant," John Ringling said many times.

At first his brothers disagreed.

"We need horses," said Al. "We can buy several good horses for what an elephant would cost."

"An elephant eats too much," said Otto. "We can't buy an elephant until we have money enough to feed him."

Then the brothers heard about a

circus owner who wanted to sell two elephants for a small price because he needed money.

"It's time to buy elephants," said John.

The five brothers began to shout and argue. John shouted the loudest of all. "Every circus needs elephants!" he yelled.

Otto listened quietly. Then he said, "Maybe John is right. Let's buy the elephants."

That settled it. If Otto was willing to spend the money for elephants, it must be the right thing to do. The Ringlings bought Babe and Fannie, the first of the many elephants in their circus.

Babe and Fannie followed the band in the circus parades. They helped pull the ropes to lift the tent before

each performance. They carried the heavy tent poles to the wagons for loading when it was time to move on to the next town. Then they walked mile after mile behind the wagons.

It began to rain hard one night as the wagons moved along a dirt road. The rain turned the dirt to mud.

"Now I know why a circus is called a mud show," Charlie grumbled. "It's because we have to travel through the mud so many times."

A wagon driver called, "Wagon Number Three hit a mudhole. One of the back wheels is stuck in the mud."

"Wagon Number Five is stuck in the mud!" another driver called.

Teams of horses struggled to pull

the wagons from the mire. The wagon wheels sank deeper into the mud.

"Get the elephants!" Charlie ordered.

A helper led Babe and Fannie forward. Babe pushed her big head against the back of one wagon, and Fannie leaned against the other wagon. Soon both wagons were out of the mudholes.

The rain stopped. The wagon train moved ahead. Babe and Fannie each got an extra bale of hay that night for having worked so hard.

Chapter 8

Sunday School Circus

For the first six years, the Ringling Brothers Circus was a mud show. After that, the circus had made enough money to travel by train. This was much more comfortable than riding in bumpy wagons, and much faster too! Even the elephants rode in railroad cars made especially for them.

The Ringling brothers hired many more performers to work for them. They hired bareback riders, tightrope walkers, acrobats, and clowns. They also hired wild animal trainers, who brought their own bears, lions, and tigers to the show.

However, by this time there were many other circuses. Some of these shows allowed thieves and pickpockets to roam about freely through the large crowds gathered on the circus grounds. As the crowd moved about before the show, it was easy for the pickpockets to steal wallets and watches. Also the ticket sellers for many shows refused to give the customers the right change when they bought tickets.

"Papa taught us to be honest men," Al Ringling told his brothers. "We will never knowingly allow pickpockets at our circus."

Soon after that, a dishonest man tried to join the Ringling Brothers Circus.

"I'll pay you a few dollars every month if you'll let me sell tickets," he said to Charlie, who was general manager at that time.

Charlie shook his head. He knew what the man intended to do.

"I won't take very much from the customers," the man said eagerly. "If a man gives me a 5-dollar bill for a 50-cent ticket, I'll hand him at least three dollars in change."

Charlie's face reddened with anger. "Get off this circus lot and don't come back," he told the man. "We run an honest show. We won't have your kind of person around here."

The two other Ringling brothers, Gus and Henry, finally joined the circus. Gus was assigned to move ahead of the show with the crews that put up posters and billboard signs. Henry was placed at the door to watch all the ticket sellers and to make sure the customers got the right change.

The Ringlings also hired detectives and policemen. Nobody had to worry about having his wallet stolen at a Ringling performance.

Because the Ringling show was clean and honest, it soon became known as the "Sunday School Circus."

"Get your tickets here, ladies and gentlemen," the ticket sellers cried before each performance. "Step right this way and buy your tickets!"

Men, women, and children moved through the opening to the animal tent. They bought peanuts to feed the elephants. They gazed at long-necked giraffes and at the squat, fat hippopotamus which seemed to have

no neck at all. They were a bit frightened when they walked beside the cages of the "big cats," as the lions and tigers were called.

They had to hurry along, for there were so many animals to see before the circus performance! Then they went into the main tent, for the show was about to begin.

The band was playing bright, brassy music as the crowd gathered. There was an extra trombone player with the band tonight. Charlie Ringling had decided to put on a bandsman's scarlet and gold uniform to play with the band, as he still did once in a while.

Alf T. sat in the front row with several newspaper reporters.

"I can give you lots of good stories to write about the show!" he told the reporters. "This year's circus is the biggest and the best we have ever had!"

One of the reporters laughed. "You say that every year, Mr. Ringling," the reporter said.

A slender man in a black coat and shining black boots stepped into the center ring. This was Al Ringling, director of the show. He bowed to the audience. Then he blew a shrill blast on a silver whistle as a signal for the performance to begin.

First came the grand entry, when all the performers and animals went along the sawdust trail around the inside of the tent. Young men in white tunics banded in gold stood in golden chariots pulled by horses with flowing manes. Striped zebras trotted along smartly behind the floats on which the clowns were riding. Pretty

girls in bright costumes rode on the elephants' heads.

A box of seats near the center ring remained empty until the grand entry was finished. Then a tall, heavyset young man with dark, curly hair entered the box. Following him were several people wearing evening clothes. John Ringling, whose job was to plan the routes taken by the circus, seldom had time to attend a performance. When he did, he always brought important people with him. His guests tonight included the mayor of the town and the governor of the state!

John waved his gold-headed cane in greeting to his brother Al, but Al was too busy to notice. Al had a long black whip in his hand. He blew a shrill blast on the whistle and cracked the whip. Into the ring stepped the famous liberty horses, trained to work alone.

The band played a different kind of music now. The horses seemed to dance forward and then backward in time to the music. Actually the bandsmen were playing very carefully so that their music was in time to the rhythm set by the horses' dancing feet.

Al cracked the whip again.

The liberty horses bent their front legs to bow to the audience. They waited for the applause, then trotted off to the place where their handlers waited for them.

In the ring at one end of the tent, trained bears rode bicycles. Four seals flippered into the ring at the other end of the tent. They tossed big red balls into the air with their

noses. One seal played the tune of "Yankee Doodle" by blowing into a set of silver horns.

A big cage had been raised in the center ring. Lions and tigers entered the cage from a small chute at the side. They roared and growled. They struck out with their paws at the trainer who was in the cage with them. But they climbed up on high stools, one by one. They sat quietly as the trainer opened the jaws of a huge lion on the ground below them and even put his head inside the open jaws for a moment.

The show moved on at a fast pace. Otto Ringling stood near the tent opening to watch the last part of the performance. He looked up at the trapeze artists swinging high in the air in their spangled costumes.

He watched the bareback riders, the jugglers, the acrobats, and the clowns.

Otto's eyes moved slowly around the tent. He found the faces of his brothers and saw their smiles of pride. He shared the feeling with them.

The Ringling brothers had come a long way since that damp dawn in McGregor, Iowa, when the circus boat edged to the dock. The brothers had worked hard as a team to build a great circus from boyhood dreams. But it had been worth the struggle.

The reward was here in the circus tent. It shone in the happy faces of the audience. The Ringling brothers were bringing joy and excitement into the lives of many people. There could be no greater reward than that, for that was what a circus was all about.

Afterword

In building their circus, the Ringling brothers also made a great deal of money. They used it to buy smaller shows to add to their own.

Twenty years after the Ringling boys opened their circus in Baraboo, they were paying salaries to over 1,000 performers and workmen. They owned 350 of the world's finest horses and a herd of 30 elephants.

But the Barnum and Bailey Circus was even bigger. It had more performers, more horses, and more elephants. The brothers were aware of this, and they were determined that their show would be the biggest and the best.

Three years later, the Ringlings had a chance to buy the Barnum and Bailey Circus. Mr. Barnum and Mr. Bailey had died. Mrs. Bailey managed the circus, and she was eager to sell. The Ringling brothers bought the Barnum and Bailey Circus. Now they were truly the circus kings of America!

The shows were managed separately for many years. Then in 1919 they were combined under the name "Ringling Bros. and Barnum & Bailey Circus."

The five Ringling brothers have been dead for many years now. But the circus, which still bears their name, takes to the road each season. Circus performances can be seen on television. Many motion pictures have been made about the circus, and several circus museums have been built to honor the Ringlings.

The Ringling brothers' best memorial, however, is the circus itself. The five boys' dream still lives on in what is billed as "The Greatest Show on Earth."